Globalization
and
Theology

Other books in this series:

HORIZONS IN THEOLOGY

Globalization and Theology

JOERG RIEGER

Abingdon Press
Nashville

GLOBALIZATION AND THEOLOGY

Copyright © 2010 by Joerg Rieger

All rights reserved.

This book is printed on acid-free paper.

Library of Congress Cataloging-in-Publication Data

Rieger, Joerg.
    Globalization and theology / Joerg Rieger.
        p. cm. — (Horizons in theology)
    Includes bibliographical references and index.
    ISBN 978-1-4267-0065-1 (trade pbk. : alk. paper)
    1. Globalization—Religious aspects—Christianity. 2. Theology. I. Title.
    BR115.G59R54 2010
    261.8—dc22

                                                                    2010005525

10 11 12 13 14 15 16 17 18 19—10 9 8 7 6 5 4 3 2 1

MANUFACTURED IN THE UNITED STATES OF AMERICA

CONTENTS

INTRODUCTION

Globalization is one of the catchwords of our time, often referring to the economic, political, and cultural phenomena that have come to affect every part of the globe. Although there are competing models of globalization, as we shall see, globalization is often discussed in its dominant forms, like for instance the spread of global corporations and how they shape the economies of whole countries, and the proliferation of free-trade agreements that are supposed to ease the flow of goods and money from one country to another. Globalization is also discussed in terms of the political alliances and tensions between countries, most visibly expressed in wars that are being fought at all times in a globalizing world, and it is discussed in terms of the impact on cultures, which are changing sometimes rapidly, often under the influence of those cultures that benefit from economic and political globalization.

What is often overlooked, however, is that ever since it emerged in the globalizing world of the Roman Empire, Christian theology has had its own unfolding history of globalization. Consequently, Christian theology and globalization are not two separate subjects. They are organically intertwined rather than artificially connected. That theology has commonly failed to understand the inextricable connections between theology and globalization is one of the problems that will be addressed in this book.

As we investigate Christian theology and globalization together, it will become clear that theology can no longer be understood without globalization. Processes of globalization influenced theology from the very beginning—consider only

1

that the New Testament was written in the language of an earlier globalization process (Greek) rather than in the language that Jesus and the earliest disciples spoke (Aramaic). Equally important for our topic, however, is that globalization can ultimately not be understood without theology.

Many readers interested in theology will expect this book to be a theological response to globalization, but no such response can be envisioned until we realize how theology itself is part of the processes of globalization, for good or for ill. Readers interested in matters of globalization may expect this book to make some theological argument for or against globalization, but no such argument can be put forth unless it is understood how processes of globalization are inextricably related to theological developments. This book begins, therefore, by dealing with the many intersections of economic, political, cultural, and theological globalization, which go unnoticed for the most part.

COMPLEXITY

One of the dangers in dealing with globalization and theology has to do with reductionism. The authors of the *Global Transformations Reader* warn about this: "To reduce globalization to a purely economic or technological logic is . . . profoundly misleading since it ignores the inherent complexity of the forces that shape modern societies and world order."[1] This is, no doubt, an important insight, which we will pursue in this book. Nevertheless, the problem for scholars of theology and religion has to do with the other extreme, for the most part, since here the worlds of ideas, symbols, and even religious practices are often dealt with in abstraction from economic and technological phenomena. In this book, we will therefore have to push beyond another sort of reductionism that limits theological reflection in its own ways, and engaging the globalization debate is one way to accomplish this.

Whereas invoking matters of complexity often becomes an escape from dealing with the most pressing issues, which in the con-

2

text of globalization are closely linked to economic and political pressures, an awareness of the complexity of both globalization and theology can also help identify alternatives. The good news to be kept in mind, in this context, is that globalization is not a unified phenomenon; if it were, this book would be telling a story of things becoming constantly and invariably more identical. Theology would be on the way to becoming a uniform phenomenon, where everyone would be expected to think exactly alike. Moreover, if globalization were a unified phenomenon, the dominant moves in economics, politics, and culture could be expected to be in untroubled harmony with theological developments and vice versa.

Although it is indeed often the case that dominant economics, politics, culture, and theology go hand in hand, in this book I will examine alternative forms of globalization as well. The dominant forms of globalization tend to move from the top down, resulting in concentrations of power in the hands of fewer and fewer people, and large sectors of theology have been quick to follow suit, mostly without being aware of how their approaches imitate the top-down moves of dominant globalization. Alternative forms of globalization often tend to move in the opposite direction—from the bottom up and including broader groups of people—and the exciting thing is that some theologies have been at the forefront of these movements. In these cases, the level of awareness of the challenges of globalization (and thus the epistemological horizon) is much greater, since alternatives within a dominant context need to be embraced consciously; "going with the flow" is, for the most part, not an option here.

As we shall see, the dominant forms of globalization often proceed by erasing and eliminating alternatives. Alternative forms of globalization not only resist this move and encourage diversity but also encourage fresh visions of unity in diversity. To paraphrase the German biblical scholar Ernst Käsemann, the New Testament canon itself is the basis of the diversity of the church rather than its monochromatic unity. The same could be said for the highly diverse body of writings that is contained in what Christians call the Old Testament. Not surprisingly, some Christian theologians who are deeply worried about the challenge of this sort of diversity have suggested that the biblical canon itself might be part of the problem.

In what follows, we approach the topic of globalization and theology in terms of its history. Although this history itself is complex, with many twists and turns, certain patterns emerge that will help us understand the bigger picture and the challenges that haunt us in our contemporary situation.

EVALUATION

A final caveat: just as globalization itself is a complex phenomenon, so is the evaluation of it. Moralizing accounts that focus on intention are the least helpful here, as they usually attribute less-than-pristine intentions to the other side. Nevertheless, even the harshest globalizers were generally well intentioned and felt they were doing the right thing: the Romans claimed that their empire would bring peace (the *pax romana*) and a better life, the crusaders of the Middle Ages fought for salvation and liberation, and neoliberal capitalism promises the future happiness of all. That processes of globalization are commonly underwritten by the best of intentions is more than a marketing ploy.

In this context, Christian theologians need to raise different questions: how do these various embodiments of globalization measure up to how we understand the divine as embodied in core Judeo-Christian traditions and in the person and work of Jesus Christ? More specifically, what kind of power is at work here, and how is it related to how different theologies envision divine power? These questions are at the core of the disagreements between the various theological ways of dealing with globalization that are presented in the following.

One more question needs to be raised, wondering what contributions these various embodiments of globalization make to true human well-being and the well-being of the world, which God loves (John 3:16). Jesus himself presented this criterion to his followers: "You will know them by their fruits" (Matt. 7:16).

CHAPTER ONE

GLOBALIZATION, THEOLOGY, AND HARD POWER

I t is often forgotten today that globalization is not without
precedent. A look at history tells us that globalization is an
old phenomenon, which is closely connected to the emergence of a variety of empires in human history. While empires
come in different forms and shapes, they share in common the
effort to expand their reach as far as possible, geographically and
otherwise, and to bring all of life under their control.[1] Such control can be exercised in various ways, as we will see, but one of
the most common forms of control is hard power.

Globalization, in this context, means the expansion of control
primarily through the use of hard power over an ever larger geo-
graphical area, linked to the expansion of control over more and
more aspects of life—not only economic and political but also
cultural, religious, personal, emotional, and so on. This sort of
globalization can be defined in terms of the expansion of top-
down power at all levels of life, of mounting power differentials,
of suppression of alternatives at all levels, and in terms of a concomitant erasure of local difference. This erasure of difference
happens at the cultural level, as is often noted; for instance, as

traditional ways of life and of thinking are abandoned. Nevertheless, this erasure of difference even manifests itself in the erasure of biological diversity, both past and present. For example, the Romans deeply influenced ecological circuits when they deforested large coastal regions in order to build their fleets. The landscape of the Mediterranean coasts still bears the marks of these actions. The goal of this sort of globalization is control over as much of the world and over as large a part of reality as possible, and one of the results is a growing gap between those on the top and those on the bottom, between the rich and the poor. Top-down globalization, in its various manifestations, creates concentrations of power and wealth in the hands of a few, to the detriment of the majority of people.

The Roman Empire will serve as our first example, as it provides the context in which Christianity was born—a context that deeply influenced Judeo-Christian traditions. The centralization of the Roman government under Gaius Julius Caesar constituted a major step in the Roman transition from being a republic to becoming an empire. In the process, power and wealth became even more concentrated at the top. The birth of Jesus occurred during the reign of the first official Roman emperor, Augustus, only a few decades later. This setting is important because the influence of empire extends to all aspects of life, and so it is not surprising that the Jesus movement ran into conflicts with the status quo and with all those who saw no alternative but to adapt to it. At the heart of these conflicts was the question of power and its theological justification: was divine power located at the top, with the various elites, or was divine power at work at the bottom, with the people—where the Jesus movement kept building?

The tensions between the Roman Empire, its supporters, and emerging Christianity can be seen in many of the writings of the New Testament, though only between the lines or in coded language. The writers needed to be cautious, as the influence of the Roman Empire was all-pervasive not just in the days of Jesus but also in their own time, in the latter parts of the first century. The writers of the Gospels, for instance, narrate the involvement of the Roman authorities in Jesus' crucifixion in slightly different ways, some of them more cautious than others. Nevertheless, they all preserve a "dangerous memory" of the fact that Jesus had been a threat to the aspirations of the empire.

In this context, politics and religion as well as the various actors are inextricably connected: the Roman Empire is not only represented by Pontius Pilate, the Roman governor, but also by the Jewish high priests, who were appointed by the Roman governors, and by vassals of Roman power such as Herod and his people.[2] The hard power of the Roman Empire, which was brought to bear with special force in unruly and faraway provinces, was at work through all of these channels. Direct military exercises, brutal devastation of whole communities, and massacres were not uncommon; some of these manifestations of empire were mirrored in the life of Jesus. Soon after Jesus' birth, the Gospel of Matthew reports, Herod ordered the killing of all children in the area of Bethlehem in order to get rid of what might become a threat to his power. This way of terrorizing and traumatizing the population had consequences, one of which is still prevalent in the contemporary world in migrant and refugee communities: Jesus' family, too, was forced to migrate to Egypt as refugees (Matt. 2:13-18).

Keeping in mind this inextricable relation of religion and politics, Jesus' proverbial response to paying taxes must be seen in a new light: the advice to "give to the emperor the things that are the emperor's, and to God the things that are God's" is often referenced as if Jesus were arguing for a peaceful coexistence of empire and religion, as if the emperor would be the ruler of things political and God would be the ruler of things religious. But Jesus can hardly be accused of forgetting what every Jew knew, namely that God could never be relegated to the religious realm (an idea which, in essence, is a modern invention), leaving the political realm to the emperor. All three Gospels that report this story mention that the context of Jesus' advice was a trap—set by both religious and political adversaries (as Mark and Matthew note). Luke emphasizes that they were amazed that they were not able to trap Jesus "in the presence of the people." The people, therefore, must have gotten this deeper meaning, what James Scott has called the "hidden transcripts," which are an important part of the "arts of resistance"[3] (see Luke 20:20-26). The globalizing empire's strategy of erasing local difference appears not to have worked in this situation.

These tensions with the hard power of the Roman Empire continued and intensified after Jesus' execution, supporting the impression that the Crucifixion cannot be seen as a one-time mistake of the empire. Early Christianity stood in sharp contrast with the emperor cult, which directed religious worship toward the emperor and was a much more significant part of the overall structure of the Roman Empire than theological scholarship has realized.[4] The early Christian confession that "Jesus is Lord" was a direct challenge to the power of the empire, which held that the emperor was lord. Other statements of the Christian faith implied as much: confessing Jesus as savior when the emperor was considered savior, proclaiming faith in—and therefore allegiance to—Jesus when the object of faith was the emperor, and claiming that Jesus was the Son of God when the emperor was considered the son of the divine could not go unnoticed. Other language would have been available for Jesus, but it seems that Paul was not interested in using it.

It should be clear by now that a merely religious explanation of these tensions will not suffice. The Romans were religiously quite tolerant and managed to include gods of other religions, like the Egyptian gods Isis and Osiris, in their worship. In a globalizing world, both then and now, those in power often do not mind some diversion when their interests are not challenged. What cannot be tolerated, however, are real alternatives, such as the ones that were provided by early Christianity. Whereas there might have been some well-defined space in Roman minds for other lords, saviors, and divine sons who were willing to play along with the power of the emperor, what was unacceptable was to put Jesus in such a place of power. A day laborer in construction from Galilee who led a movement of the common people and who ended up on one of the crosses of the empire—Paul kept reminding his constituents of this cross—could not easily be assimilated by the empire and its concentration of power in the hands of a few.

The tolerance of those who seek to rule the world from the top down, via hard power, can only go so far: they cannot accept the existence of real alternatives, and they are unable to incorporate in their globalizing schemes alternative sorts of power—particularly the ones that move from the bottom up and thus counter the typical top-down movement of empires' aspirations to global domination. If the control of the Roman Empire was to be maintained, the control of the emperor needed to be maintained as well. The whole theological apparatus of the Roman Empire was designed to maintain this sort of control, and imagining God's power in terms of the power of the emperor was crucial.

Unlike the confession of the lordship of Jesus, the principles of classical theism matched the requirements of the empire and provided valuable support for its goals. Classical theism envisioned God not only as all-powerful but also as immutable and impassible, qualities that were designed to affirm unilateral and top-down power. The divine would be less than all-powerful, and its top-down power would be compromised, if anything were in a position to affect it, touch it, or change it. The Nicene Creed, produced in the fourth century at the initiative and under the oversight of the first Christian emperor, Constantine, has often been read in this light. If Jesus is of the same substance as God, as Constantine proposed to the Nicene Council and as the Council affirmed in the Nicene Creed, the question is how God is envisioned. If God is envisioned in the terms of classical theism and thus in terms of the top-down power of the elites, Jesus can now also be envisioned in these terms and thus as a supporter of the top-down power of the empire.

Even the form of the Nicene Creed, the first so-called ecumenical creed, bears the stamp of the globalization efforts of the Roman Empire: this is the first time that Christian theology finds expression in the form of universal imperial decrees. While the New Testament canon witnesses to the diversity of the early church and to what might be called "unity in diversity," the Nicene Creed presents a different model. At the Council of

Nicaea, the church adopted the procedures by which the empire hammered out its decrees: a unified council that was called, funded, and led by the emperor made the decisions. Presiding over the Council of Nicaea, Constantine proposed the central theological term of the Nicene Creed: the *homoousia* (essential sameness) of God and Jesus, the first and the second person of the Trinity. With the Council of Nicaea, the church entered a process of globalization that was qualitatively different from what had gone before. Nevertheless, these efforts at globalization were not entirely successful, and there are alternative ways to interpret the Nicene Creed, as we will see in the next chapter.

The power that drives all these forms of globalization is of a hard sort and clearly top-down. The Roman military exploits and conquests designed to expand the empire as far as possible are well known, but similar force was applied within the confines of the empire. Jesus was one of many others who were crucified—this was a preferred way for executing political rebels. This method of execution demonstrated the power of the Roman Empire over its subjects and their communities. The Romans would crucify as many as two thousand people on a single day in one area. The terror that such events must have struck in the population is hard to imagine. Crucifixions and other harsh forms of execution, such as using people as human torches for parties given by those in positions of power, were means of executing Christians long after Christ's death, and even the Apostle Paul seems to have been executed by similar methods.

Remembering the fact that Paul spent his life in and out of Roman prisons, we cannot consider his fate—like the fate of Jesus—as a mistake of the empire either. The sort of local difference that was supposed to be erased here was indeed dangerous, as it held real promise of providing broad-based alternatives and thus presented a challenge to the empire. Hard, top-down power, held in the hands of a few, needs to draw clear lines in order to maintain its force with the masses, even if it may show some tolerance within these lines.

Another example of a sort of globalization that proceeds via hard power and from the top down is the Spanish conquest. Here, too, theology and globalization go hand in hand. Columbus sailed westward in the firm belief that it was the will of God to expand the reach of the Spanish Empire. After the Spanish had set foot in the New World in order to take possession of it, it was Pope Alexander VI who in 1493 endorsed the reign over this world by Spanish emperors, who carried the title "Holy Roman Emperor." Critics of this move have often claimed that the main purpose for this sort of globalization was greed. Gustavo Gutiérrez, for instance, has proposed that the alternative before the conquistadors was "God or gold."

It must not be overlooked, however, that the conquistadors held strong theological concerns of their own, and that the pope's endorsement cannot be reduced to the matter of greed either. The conquest was guided not merely by hunger for wealth and power but also by particular images of God as heavenly monarch who, through the Roman Catholic Church, endorsed the earthly monarchies of the Spaniards and Portuguese both at home and abroad, and by a particular sense of mission.

The hard power that was brought to bear in the conquest is firmly established by the history books. The natives of the Americas were enslaved with such effectiveness that millions of them died—amounting to genocide. Even cautious estimates put the population of the colonized territories at seventy million before the Spaniards arrived, and at ten million in 1625.[5] Any resistance was brutally repressed, and in the early years of the conquest the conquistadors killed hundreds of thousands of people, often using the cruelest methods imaginable, such as slitting open people's stomachs and burning their chiefs alive in public. Even the missionary work that went hand in hand with conquest reflects the use of hard power, though in a very particular way, as the leading theologians of conquest, writing in Spain, did not want to extend the methods of conquest directly to missionary conversion. As a result, they did not permit the conversion of the natives by force.

War as direct means of conversion was rejected not only by opponents of the conquest, like Bartolomé de Las Casas, but also by the theologians who supported the conquest—thinkers as

11

different as Juan Gines de Sepulveda and Tomas de Vitoria, the latter of whom laid important foundations for modern law. The use of the means of war was only permitted when the natives put up resistance to the proclamation of the gospel. In other words, hard power was permissible when the natives sought to assert and maintain their local differences, which might have provided alternatives to the Christianity promoted by the Spanish and, by extension, to Spanish imperial rule. As long as real alternatives could be suppressed in this way, the missionaries would prove to be successful.

This approach throws some light on the often-observed phenomenon that the conversion of the Native Americans to Christianity was only skin-deep. Underneath the adopted Christian faith, they were able to maintain some of their traditions, an arrangement that resulted in hybridized religious images. Yet such arrangements may not be unusual for situations of grave power differentials based on hard, top-down power, where the elites in power do not need to be overly concerned about micromanaging people's lives. As long as the mass of the people conform to commonly accepted standards in public—for the Spaniards these standards were contained in Christianity—the empire appears to be secure.

There may be somewhat of an analogy here to the contemporary situation where capitalism does not appear to be too concerned about micromanaging as long as people accept its fundamental principles. From the perspective of marketing and advertising, it may even be advantageous if people embody the basic principles of capitalism in such a way that they adapt them to their own cultural activities. Local differences in such a situation not only pose no threat but also can be used in order to influence more people more effectively. It may be easier to influence Hispanics in the United States, for instance, if advertisements geared to their taste appear in Spanish language.

More enlightened forms of top-down power, especially when they are securely held by powerful groups such as corps of Spanish conquistadors or global corporations, know that there are some advantages to picking people up where they are. The mestizo culture in the south of the Americas, which allowed for mixture and mingling despite clearly arranged hierarchies (maintained via degrees of mixture and whether people were born in Spain or the New World), may be another example for this attitude. Conversely, if local differences are successfully integrated into the system, they no longer provide a challenge. The food court at the mall, with its culinary diversity, exemplifies this sort of domestication in an extreme sort of way.

One final form of globalization from the top down via hard power that must be addressed is the modern phenomenon of fascism. Here, too, theology and the process of globalization go hand in hand. German fascism, for example, is fundamentally misunderstood if it is seen as the work of a secular group of power-brokers. The Swiss theologian Karl Barth understood the problem at stake in this situation when, at the beginning of his *Church Dogmatics*, he defined the task of theology as the struggle of Christian faith against distorted Christian faith, rather than as the struggle against atheism and those who did not claim faith. The Barmen Declaration of 1934 of the German Confessing Church, of which Barth was the principal author, opposed the use of Christianity and religion for the purposes of fascism. Its purpose was not to challenge a lack of faith, but to reject the distorted Christian faith that had come to endorse a fascist ideology and the rule of the few over the many, even in the church.[6]

German fascism is well remembered for wielding hard power. War, for instance, was considered a legitimate part of politics in relation to other countries. Within the nation, hard power manifested itself in growing prison populations, a move that was supposed to keep the streets "safe" not only from those who posed criminal threats but also from those who embodied real alternatives. Six million Jews were killed in German concentration camps, as is often remembered, but another six million people were also killed in these camps—all of them because they were different from the fascist image of the ideal German—including gays, lesbians, and gypsies, as well as socialists, communists, and union leaders. The secret service was everywhere, using any available method to spread terror, including torture. The soldiers who were fighting Germany's expansionist wars wore belt buckles that said, "God with us" (*Gott mit uns*), and were supported by an army of chaplains, who in turn were supported and encouraged by the churches in whose sanctuaries the swastikas and other symbols of national pride were proudly displayed.

This marriage of top-down power and Christianity is now deeply questioned in Europe, and this may be in part the reason for the skeptical attitude against Christianity that is often found in European countries. It is always surprising to Europeans that a similar attitude is by and large lacking in the United States, where Christianity still enthusiastically supports war and other expressions of hard power. In Germany there are no flags to be found in churches anymore, and while the range of the German army has recently been extended again, with the lifting of a decades-old ban that prohibited the German army to operate outside of German borders, it is hard to imagine the public prayer, "God bless our troops."

To be sure, Christian theology was not merely used here against its will. It often related positively to fascist ideas and their elitist agendas, as the theological literature of the time shows: a prominent theologian like Karl Heim, for instance, compared the leadership qualities of Jesus and Hitler favorably. Heim argued that the presence of a strong leader serves as a reminder that we are not able to lead ourselves. Theology is part and parcel of this approach, notes Heim: "If we live our life under the leadership of another, we have put in his hand even our knowledge of ultimate things."[7] The proud proclamation of German Reichsbishop Ludwig Müller (whom Hitler selected) that he believed in all the doctrines must be considered in this background as well. Doctrinal orthodoxy was obviously no guarantee that Christianity would stay a course different from the powers that be.

CHAPTER TWO

GLOBALIZATION AND THEOLOGIES PROVIDING ALTERNATIVES TO HARD POWER

Whereas the above account of globalization and theology points to a troubling legacy, especially in light of the tremendous cost to human flourishing and the environment that each of these embodiments of globalization has incurred, there have been alternatives from the very beginning. While hundreds of millions of people have been killed by top-down forms of globalization during the past two thousand years—representing only the tip of the iceberg of harmful social relations that have found embodiment in harmful ecological relations[1]—there have also been more constructive and benevolent forms of globalization, supported by alternative forms of theology.

As we discuss these alternatives, please note that they emerge in the midst of the struggle against hard forms of power. In the context of an unending succession of top-down forms of globalization, which seek to expand as far as possible into the world that is known to them, there is no neutral space or safe distance from which people can operate. The postmodern feeling that there is no more "outside" to our world describes the reality of top-down forms of globalization, especially for its victims. Although this feeling has intensified in the current situation, earlier manifestations of empire were able to create similar impressions. Of course, there are always those who feel that they have some personal freedom and space—especially the ones who have some power in the system—but this may have more to do with artificial bubbles and correlated illusions than with a realistic assessment of a globalizing world.

Since the alternatives to top-down globalization to be discussed here emerge in the midst of pressure, imperfections and contradictions should not be surprising. Struggles for life and death leave little room for perfection and perfectionism. Building alternative movements is hard in such a situation, yet this seems precisely what Jesus did and what made him dangerous. Unlike others who made short-term impressions through the use of symbolic violence, or by hurling strong words at the powers that be, Jesus built a movement in which the last would indeed become the first and the first the last by forming circles of solidarity driven by the challenge of unflinching commitment: "No one who puts a hand to the plow and looks back is fit for the kingdom of God" (Luke 9:62).

Furthermore, emerging in the midst of top-down power, alternative movements like the Jesus movement are subject to constant pressure and threats. According to the Gospel of Mark, Jesus' healing of a man with a "withered" hand on a Sabbath early in Jesus' ministry results in an effort by the representatives from various branches of the status quo of the empire—the Herodians and the Pharisees—to kill Jesus (Mark 3:1-6). Jesus' famous announcement in the Gospel of Luke that the Spirit of God anointed him "to bring good news to the poor" and that he was sent to "proclaim release to the captives and recovery of sight to the blind, to let the oppressed go free, to proclaim the year of the Lord's favor" (Luke 4:18-19) did not have a very happy ending. After initial amazement and praise by the audience, the story ends in Jesus being driven out of town and a rather crass effort to "hurl him off the cliff" (Luke 4:28-30).

Despite these pressures and challenges, however, the Jesus movement saw its mission expand, sometimes in unexpected ways. At one point, Jesus learns one of the most crucial lessons for an alternative movement of globalization from a foreigner—who also happens to be a woman. Jesus first turns away the Syrophoenician woman, a Gentile who implores Jesus to perform an exorcism on her daughter, noting that the "children's food" should not be thrown "to the dogs." Her comeback that even the dogs get the children's crumbs from the table not only subverts Jesus' terms but appears to effect a mind-change in him, so that he ends up granting her wish (Mark 7:24-30).

A new sort of globalization emerges here that counters the top-down moves of the Roman Empire from its inception: this sort of globalization ties together those under pressure and gives them hope. There is no doubt: the two forms of globalization, one from the top and one from the bottom, do not go together, and it is no accident that Jesus rejects the devil's offer to rule over "all the kingdoms of the world and their splendor" (Matt. 4:8-10).

The principal divisions at work here, as Richard Horsley has pointed out, are not between "Romans" and "Jews," but between the people and the elites, the latter group including the Jewish high priests and the Herodians.[2] In this context, religious images become a highly contested ground, as Jewish images can both contribute to the globalization of the Roman Empire and point to alternative globalizations. The result is a life-and-death cultural struggle in which top-down hard power uses every available means to assimilate cultural and religious images and to erase real alternatives. This is why Jesus' struggles to renew Jewish religion had to be taken seriously. History shows that the clash of these two very different modes of globalization had consequences: Jesus was executed by an alliance of the elites. Yet this execution was not the end but the beginning of an ongoing struggle between Christianity and the Roman Empire that would last a long time.

As we have already seen, when Paul called Jesus "Lord" he made use of one of the key titles of the Roman emperor. Using this title in such a politically charged setting would only make sense if it were deliberately subversive, especially since other titles would have been readily available. Paul, whose life was in constant danger, must have known what was at stake. The only reason to call Jesus "Lord" was to point out the difference between Jesus and the emperor: Paul must have seen Jesus modeling a different sort of leadership and a different kind of power.[3]

The sort of leadership Jesus as Lord provided implies a radical break with the globalizing forces of the Roman Empire and initiates a different globalization process, namely, from below. Whereas the Roman emperor led from the top down, Paul understood that Jesus led from the bottom up: "Though he was in the form of God, [he] did not regard equality with God as something to be exploited, but emptied himself, taking the form of a slave, being born in human likeness" (Phil. 2:6-7). Paul thus proclaimed "Christ crucified, a stumbling block to Jews and foolishness to Gentiles, but to those who are the called, both Jews and Greeks, Christ the power of God and the wisdom of God" (1 Cor. 1:23-24). The fundamental conflict here is not between "Judaism" and Christianity, or between "Hellenism" and Christianity, but between two different ways of life, which amount to two different forms of globalization.

This alternative mission is reflected in the theologically charged notion of election. "God chose what is foolish in the world to shame the wise; God chose what is weak in the world to shame the strong; God chose what is low and despised in the world, things that are not, to reduce to nothing things that are" (1 Cor. 1:27-28). Here the sort of globalization from below, which was characteristic of the Jesus movement, continues and expands. Note that this form of globalization has nothing to do with the dominant model. It must not be understood as a harmless variation, as merely broadening or enriching the top-down model. It is not about adding the foolish, the weak, the lowly, and the despised to the status quo. This new form of globalization resists and counteracts globalization from above. It shames the wise and the strong, "reducing to nothing" globalization from above. All of this is, according to Paul, God's choice—God's "election," to use the technical theological term.

Christ's power as Lord, as Paul describes it, decidedly moves from the bottom up and generates a new way of being in the world. This is the power that has proved potent enough to spread to "all nations" and is projected to last "to the end of the age" (Matt. 28:19-20). Appropriating and reversing an old imperial image of society as a body, Paul makes two important points (1 Cor. 12): the church as the body of Christ models a situation where power does not demand the destruction of difference, unlike globalization from the top; but difference as such is not enough. Even the Roman Empire was willing to endorse difference to some extent, as long as it did not challenge power differentials. Paul's image of the body promotes an alternative vision of power: "God has so arranged the body, giving the greater honor to the inferior member" (1 Cor. 12:24). Globalization from below ultimately demands nothing less than the tearing down of top-down power differentials and reconstructing society and the church from below.

The clash between globalization from above and globalization from below is perennial, and so it is not surprising that it shows up in the traditions of the early church as well. In this context, however, it is pushed more and more below the surface as the church increasingly becomes part of the establishment. The Nicene Creed, for instance, formulated shortly after Christianity become the official religion of the Roman Empire in the fourth century, can be read both in terms of globalization from above and in terms of globalization from below. On the surface, this creed reflects the top-down process of globalization pursued by the emperor Constantine, who made Christianity the official religion of the Roman Empire. Religious unification was one of the strategies that Constantine pursued in order to unify the Roman Empire. In the hands of the empire, religious unification became a major tool for eradicating local differences: the heretics were exiled for the most part and their writings destroyed.

Nevertheless, the Nicene Creed can also be interpreted and appropriated in terms of a globalization from below. Constantine realized this too late, and this was perhaps the reason he later abandoned the Nicene Creed and reverted to Arianism, which upheld the absolute monarchy, singularity, and sovereignty of God. The key to reading the Nicene Creed against the grain and from the bottom up can be found in the understanding of the person of Jesus. It is striking that the Nicene Creed fails to mention something that is otherwise at the very heart of the Christian tradition: the life and ministry of Jesus. The text of the Nicene Creed moves directly from the Incarnation to the Crucifixion, as if what happened in between was of no consequence.

Here we can observe an example of the cancellation of local difference that is typical for top-down processes of globalization. The empire eradicates the narratives of Jesus' life and ministry in a specific context, at a specific time, in solidarity with the people, in order to present Jesus as a God who matches the principles of classical theism, such as impassibility, immutability, and omnipotence. The Nicene Creed contains no reference to the "local" differences of the life and ministry of a Jewish construction worker called Jesus who announced an alternative kingdom—the kingdom of God—where the last will be the first and the first will be the last (Matt. 19:30; 20:16).

In the clash between two forms of globalization, the nature of God is at stake. Constantine's design for the Council of Nicaea must have overlooked the potential alternative: as it included Jesus in the Godhead, it unwittingly opened the door to challenges to top-down ideas of God. Arius, the nemesis of the Council of Nicaea, sought to circumvent this alternative by opting for a solution that considered Jesus as a very special entity—raised far above the world and the heavens—but not quite God. When viewed through the lens of the Jesus movement, the Nicene affirmation of the divinity of Jesus challenges interpretations of God in top-down terms: as the immutable and impassible "unmoved mover" of all things.

When viewed through the lens of the Jesus movement, therefore, God would ultimately have to be rethought in terms of a relationship of equals. Reading the Nicene Creed from the bottom up—that is, from the perspective of the life and ministry of

Jesus—has radical consequences for theology: is God the one who acts from the top down and who backs up the processes of globalization from the top down, as the Christian Roman Empire, and all subsequent Christian empires to this day, believe? Or is God the one we meet in Jesus Christ, who was born in a manger in a stable rather than in a cradle in a palace, who came from a depressed area of Palestine called Galilee, who was a day laborer in construction, and who tended to side with the sick, the outcasts, and the sinners, rather than with the established and the powerful?

Resisting the efforts of top-down globalization that constantly seek to rub out these "local" differences, substantial alternatives emerge. The conservative theological positions that usually uphold the Nicene Creed never discuss these alternatives because these theological positions mostly move from the top down; by ignoring the "local" differences of Jesus' life and ministry, they end up domesticating Jesus—including his incarnation, cross, and resurrection. Whether this happens consciously or unconsciously makes no difference. At the same time, the liberal theological positions that seek to leave the Nicene Creed behind and tone down the divinity of Jesus also forego the tremendous challenge that an alternative reading of the creed poses for a globalizing church. Here the divine stays safely in heaven, unchallenged, and ready to back top-down forms of globalization. And so both conservatives and liberals fail to challenge the image of the divine that is at the core of globalization from the top down. And they fail to do what is most needed: to rethink the image of God. In this context, alternative readings of the Nicene Creed push for real alternatives as they encourage us to rethink God from the perspective of Jesus—that is, from the bottom up.

Another example for theological resistance to hard power and for an alternative model of globalization can be found in the life and work of the Spanish missionary and theologian Bartolomé de Las Casas. In this case, however, the messiness of any alternative project becomes even clearer, as Las Casas ends up unconsciously introducing another top-down model of globalization. In his theological reflections, Las Casas contrasts two forms of global-ization—what he calls "the way of Jesus Christ" and the way of the Spanish conquistadors. Whereas the conquistadors proceed with violence and warfare, he notes, Christ proceeded in a gen-tle fashion, harming no one but healing people instead, caring for them and supporting them. And while the violent globalization of the conquistadors produces fear, resentment, and death, Christ's peaceful globalization produces trust, happiness, and life.

Unlike the conquistadors, Las Casas acknowledged the humanity of the natives of the Americas; he studied their cus-toms, their religions, and their languages, and he expressed deep appreciation for them. In order to remove the reasons for violent missionary activities that went hand in hand with the conquest, Las Casas sought to create an understanding of, and sympathy for, the way of life and the religion of the Indians. Based on his stud-ies, he pointed out that the Indians were not committing idola-try and that their practice of human sacrifice was misunderstood. Nevertheless, what might be considered early beginnings of the academic fields of anthropology and religious studies, done in order to appreciate the native other, also had some downsides. In chapter 4 we have to address the fact that Las Casas maintained an assumption of the superiority of Christianity and the Spanish way of life.

What is crucial here, however, is that Las Casas managed to a certain degree to look at the Spanish world and at Christianity from the perspective of the Indians. From this point of view, he even came to realize Christ as being present in the Indians. According to Las Casas, this presence of Christ is most strongly visible in their sufferings, a recognition that has the potential to challenge the top-down approach of the Spanish conquest, which is the cause of most of these sufferings. After giving up his own privileged way of life, his *encomienda*, and his slaves, Las Casas's mission became the struggle against the top-down form of globalization embodied by the Spanish conquest, establishing alternatives that reduced the suffering of the Indians. Whereas Las Casas compared this suffering to the suffering of Christ, the problem becomes even clearer if we note that Christ's suffering was inflicted at the hands of imperial religion and the Roman Empire in his own time.

It should be clear by now that resistance against top-down forms of globalization is not just a contemporary phenomenon. The challenges presented by the organized protests to the various meetings of the World Trade Organization, beginning in Seattle in the year 2000, are reflected to some degree in Las Casas's struggles with the Spanish conquest. What is challenged in all these cases is the exercise of a sort of top-down power that misunderstands the God of Christianity, that is out of touch with the lives of the people, and that for this reason, no matter how much it insists on its benevolent intentions, invariably ends up working for the advantage of the elites. As a result, the already grave differentials in power and wealth keep growing.

A final example of theological resistance to hard power and the alternatives that grow out of such resistance can be found in theological critiques of fascism. Karl Barth's reminder of God's transcendence, echoed in the Barmen Declaration and in the German Confessing Church, must be seen in strict opposition to a theology that declared God a part of the dominant status quo. The God who is "Wholly Other" cannot be used for the justification of fascist dreams of global preeminence and dominance, no matter how benevolently they might present themselves. It is often overlooked that the fascist motto was not that Germany would destroy the world, but that the German way of life would heal the world (*"am deutschen Wesen soll die Welt genesen"*), based on the view that German achievements in all areas of culture (humanities, philosophy, sciences, and so on) would be in a position to show the way to a better life. Who could deny that this attitude is still at work in many contemporary embodiments of globalization?

Barth's notion of God as Wholly Other is more than a critique of top-down globalization processes, however. Since Barth's Wholly Other is not an abstract idea but grounded in the history of Jesus Christ, otherness is ultimately not to be equated with faceless transcendence. Divine otherness has to do with the way of Jesus Christ into the struggles, sufferings, and tensions of

23

humanity and the world. This is a lesson that Barth learned perhaps for the first time as the pastor of a church in Safenwil, Switzerland, during a union strike. While theological common sense assumed that God was on the side of the status quo, Barth began to understand that God did indeed take sides—but with the workers. The history of God in Christ provides a key example of God taking the side of the lowly and the oppressed.

Unlike the majority of his neoorthodox students, even the later Barth could never quite do away with the sense that God takes sides not only with the oppressed but also against the oppressors: "God always takes His stand unconditionally and passionately on this side and on this side alone: against the lofty and on behalf of the lowly; against those who already enjoy right and privilege and on behalf of those who are denied it and deprived of it."[4] The result of taking such a stand is a new movement, embodied in the church. Unfortunately, such sentences are buried in the depths of Barth's writings, so that many readers will never find them, and thus it is not surprising that even many Barthians are unaware of this dynamic.

Similar insights can be found in the work of Dietrich Bonhoeffer. Bonhoeffer's famous remarks about viewing things from the underside make sense in this context. Toward the end of his life, Bonhoeffer wrote those words at the end of 1942 from a German prison cell: "It remains an experience of unmatched value that we have learned to see the great events of history from the underside, from the perspective of the eliminated, the suspect, the abused, the powerless, the oppressed, and the ridiculed, in short, from the perspective of the suffering."[5] In a situation where the view from the top, from the perspective of those in positions of global power, has become so commonly accepted that it is hardly even noticed anymore, the view from below poses a fundamental challenge and a real, broad-based alternative. Bonhoeffer's logic of the underside has been taken up and developed further not only in subsequent works of Latin American liberation theologians but also elsewhere, including in the context of theology in Europe and the United States.[6]

In many strands in the Judeo-Christian traditions, God can be found in this unexpected position—on the underside. For example, when electing a people, God chooses not the powerful empire of the Egyptians, but a band of their slaves under Egyptian tutelage. God's election becomes visible in the liberation of these Hebrew slaves. This theme as a common thread carries through many of the traditions of the Bible. In the proclamations of the prophets of the Old Testament, God is once again taking the side not of those in control but of those who experience injustice and oppression. The Psalms—too often spiritualized in Christian theology—pick up similar concerns of the liberation of the oppressed, and we have already discussed the message of Jesus and Paul.

Bonhoeffer started from a similar theological insight. The underside of which he talks is not just a highly significant part of human experience that is too often neglected; the underside is where God is at work, and this is where theology needs to find its location as well. In the words of his biographer and friend Eberhard Bethge, Bonhoeffer believed that Christian theologians would have to look for God where God had already preceded us: at the underside of history.[7] If theology fails to look there, it will miss the reality of God altogether.

Keep in mind also that both Bonhoeffer and Barth not only offered critical views of globalization from above but also supported and helped shape what must be considered movements of alternative globalization. Both theologians were deeply involved with the Confessing Church in Germany, which had to operate underground because of the fact that it sought to provide true alternatives to Nazi rule. Bonhoeffer eventually joined the resistance movement against Hitler. Their failed attempt to assassinate Hitler cost Bonhoeffer his life. Barth was engaged in his own ways in the resistance against Hitler, but he also understood the importance of the struggle of the workers and remained a lifelong socialist—an important matter that is often forgotten even by those who claim an interest in his theology. In a context where capitalism claims to be the only viable option left, these theologians invite us to think and to explore other alternatives.

Although it is often assumed that the view from the underside is a recent invention of theology, this is clearly not the case. Christianity has maintained such a view from the very beginning, usually in situations of tension with the powers that be, and usually in deep connection to an understanding of Jesus Christ. From the beginning, therefore, Christianity has been involved not only with the top-down forms of globalization, but with alternative forms as well.

CHAPTER THREE

INTERLUDE: POSTCOLONIALISM, BINARIES, AND DUALISMS

Postcolonialism is a term that has gained popularity in the context of discussions of globalization and empire. Not only would this book not be complete without a short excursion in which we consider this term, but considering some of the key problems addressed by postcolonial theory will also help us get our bearings for the second half of this book.

According to one of the meanings of the term, postcolonialism emerges in the midst of the struggle with the colonial early on.[1] This reminds us that there is never a pure colonial situation without resistance and emerging alternatives. Christianity itself provides examples for this, as we have seen. Another definition understands the postcolonial as that which takes place after the official end of European colonialism, which took place at various times during the past two centuries in various locations around the globe. What both of these definitions share in common is a sense of the ongoing need for resistance. Most postcolonial theorists understand that even in postcolonial situations, after the official end of colonialism, the struggle against oppression continues. Although the times of official colonialism, with viceroys and established government apparatuses over foreign terrain, are by and large in the past, we are now dealing with what elsewhere I have called "the postcolonial empire,"[2] a phenomenon that will be discussed in the next chapter.

Postcolonial theory and other related theories have emphasized the complexity of phenomena like globalization. Dualistic schemes of oppressors and oppressed, good guys and bad guys, the rich and the poor can no longer be upheld—or so the argument goes. Since everybody is said to share in each of these categories to some degree, postcolonial thought stresses the notion of hybridity: everybody is a hybrid of oppressor and oppressed to a certain extent. Even in the classical tension between colonizer and colonized, neither side remains unaffected by the process of colonization. Nevertheless, we should add here that hybridity is in a special way the reality of those who find themselves located toward the underside of the colonial or postcolonial system, because they are hardly in positions where they can escape the impact of those in power; those in power, however, usually have more flexibility.

For the colonized, this means that they are shaped by the colonial world to such a degree that, to the casual observer, it can appear as if they are becoming more and more like the colonizers. In a colonial situation, the colonized adopt—or are forced to adopt—some of the traits of the colonizers, including their dress, their language, their culture, and even their mannerisms. One of the most important insights of postcolonial theory, however, is that they do so with a twist. The colonized never become exactly identical to the colonizers. As they mimic the colonizers, an important difference remains. The postcolonial term of *mimicry*, informed by poststructuralist philosophical observations, emphasizes the difference between the original and that which is imitated. In this difference lies the potential for subversion and ultimately for resistance.[3]

For the most part, these complex relations of colonizer and colonized are envisioned in a context of hard power, where the colonizers have substantial amounts of power over the colonized. In a situation of brutal conquest, for instance, the colonized have little choice but to adapt if they want to survive. In a mellower situation of colonialism, however, the colonized may have more leeway to express themselves, and they may have permission to continue some of their own traditions that do not pose a challenge (in many African countries, for example, the missionaries prohibited the use of drums in worship but adopted other cultural expressions). But what about a postcolonial setting? Here, multiculturalism is often embraced as a positive value, even by those who seek to uphold the status quo; people are encouraged to pursue their traditions if only for nostalgia's sake; and the fact that postcolonial societies usually have some sort of democratic government seems to point to a fundamental equality among the various groups.

There are many voices, and even some postcolonial theorists, who contend that the stark dualisms and binaries that were characteristic of situations of conquest and colonialism have disappeared in the postcolonial world. These voices celebrate notions of otherness and difference as if they had suddenly become a reality after the breakdown of the classical hard-power models of globalization such as conquest, colonialism, and fascism. But this is hardly accurate. Grave power differentials still exist in the postcolonial world and underneath the common endorsements of multiculturalism, although they may be less visible. The war of the United States against Iraq that was declared by President Bush in 2003, for instance, may have been an exception in that it brought to bear the hard power wielded by the world's most powerful military; but even that effort was not geared toward establishing a new colony: no U.S. viceroy or governor was installed and no permanent U.S. rule in Iraq was established; clearing the slate so that capitalist economic structures could take over, shape the lives of Iraqis, and manage their oil reserves was considered to be sufficient.[4] In hindsight, using nonmilitary methods and more decidedly postcolonial strategies to convert the Iraqi economy and culture might have been not only more effective but also quicker.

29

The power differentials that shape the world today are much more difficult to spot, and it is becoming even more difficult to see them from the top than ever before. Although those in traditional positions of privilege would not have been able to grasp the full horror of hard power wielded through mass crucifixions, direct military actions, mutilations of resistant bodies, gas chambers, and myriad forms of torture, they would at least have had some dim awareness of the existence of some of these things. In a postcolonial world, however, those in positions of privilege often lack even a basic awareness of the consequences of economic pressures and exploitation, such as large numbers of desperate people out of work, or hungry children—even in the United States. And those who go bankrupt or die because of lack of affordable health care and other support, usually fail and die silently behind closed doors. Moreover, reports in the media of unemployment, hunger, or lack of health care systematically ignore connections between these struggles and the interests of the postcolonial empire.

The point of my argument is that even in an age in which hard power is becoming less fashionable and when difference and multiculturalism is affirmed—in the United States this was one of the symbolic changes that happened in the transition from President George W. Bush to President Barack Obama—we need to remember that grave power differentials continue to exist. Now, however, power appears in softer forms, often couched in economic and cultural relationships, where at first sight the line between oppressors and oppressed seems to have become blurry. Nevertheless, the underlying power differentials have not disappeared; if anything, they have become more deeply entrenched. Our problem resembles what happens in the transition from physical abuse of others (spouses, children, and other dependents) to other more hidden forms of abuse on the basis of deep-seated economic, cultural, religious, and psychological dependencies.

The reason postcolonial notions like hybridity, mimicry, and ambivalence are important today is not because dualisms and binaries have finally disappeared but because grave power differentials continue to take the form of sharp dualisms and binaries. If fifty thousand people die every day from hunger and preventable causes—up from ten thousand people in 1983—are we not witnessing a dualistic situation?[5] If 225 of the world's richest individuals own as much as half of what the world's population earns in a year, how is this not another sharp dualism? And if the global economy recovers after the crash of 2008 and 2009 without a concomitant recovery of jobs—half of the jobs lost in the United States are projected to be gone forever—does this not point to a rather pronounced dualism in terms of who benefits from the economy and who does not?

Since the economy is such a major factor in the postcolonial empire, as we shall see, the often-lamented existence of grave economic differences needs to be acknowledged as a major factor in top-down globalization. The widening gap between rich and poor has become proverbial and is hardly disputed by anyone. Without playing down or neglecting the significant differences of gender, race, and ethnicity, an awareness of the substantial differences between the economic classes in our time reminds us that merely celebrating otherness and difference cannot solve the problem of top-down globalization.[6]

In other words, binaries and dualisms do not disappear in postcolonial times; rather, they continue to form the bedrock on which relationships have to be negotiated. Hybridity is based on differentials of power, not just on difference in general, and it is because of inherent power differentials that it may lead to resistance. Likewise, mimicry is only effective in situations of fairly pronounced power differentials: without power differentials, mimicry would just be another game, without direction or shape. The postcolonial notion of ambivalence, finally, also needs to be seen in this light. Ambivalence—the reminder that the powers that be are never uniform and without self-contradictions—only becomes a tool of resistance in a situation where these powers keep pushing for some kind of uniformity and for the erasure of local differences; otherwise, ambivalence would be just a frustrating and meaningless state of indecision.

The ethnocentrisms that postcolonial critics have often chal-lenged may serve as a case in point. Without the backing of the clear power differentials of a capitalist economy, even Eurocentrism would just be another ethnocentrism,[7] and Anglo culture in the United States would have to wait for the latest polls in order to find out whether it was still significant. In real-ity, Eurocentrism and the dominance of Anglo culture in the United States do not have to be too concerned about their power, as long as they continue to benefit from capitalist eco-nomic relationships. This insight also serves as a reminder of why so many Europeans and so many Anglos in the United States reap only limited benefits from buying into ethnocentric posi-tions: capitalism does not provide the same amount of support to Europeans and Anglos who do not belong to the ruling classes.

Fredric Jameson has defined globalization as "an untotalizable totality which intensifies binary relations between its parts—mostly nations, but also regions and groups. . . . Such relations are first and foremost ones of tension or antagonism, when not out-right exclusion."[8] Even the postcolonial empire maintains binary relations and dualisms—between the haves and the have-nots, between those in positions of top-down power and control and those who hold alternative forms of power, and so on—and there are efforts to produce a totality that is dominated by those in charge. What does this mean for alternative takes on globalization?

CHAPTER FOUR

GLOBALIZATION, THEOLOGY, AND SOFT POWER

In chapter 1, we observed the close connection of theology, globalization via hard power, and empire. Empires, as we have seen, have taken different forms and shapes, but they share in common efforts to bring all aspects of life under their control and to empower the few over the many. Nevertheless, it is frequently overlooked that hard power is not the only form that this control assumes. A well-meaning pastor, Bob Roberts, assuming with journalist Thomas Friedman that the "world is flat," recently wrote that Hitler was the last global leader who sought to establish global domination, and that others like Bin Laden will not succeed.[1] At this point in history, Roberts believes, we do not have to worry about grave power differentials anymore and we are now dealing with "global convergence," which brings people together without boundaries.

This may be an exceptionally naive take on the current situation, but it is not uncommon for people to jump to such conclusions. People often assume that, ever since the defeat of the British in the American Revolution, power differentials have been flattened in the United States of America. The same assumption is made for postapartheid South Africa, post-Nazi Germany, and the North American countries under the North American Free Trade Agreement (NAFTA). In this chapter, we therefore need to take a closer look at how top-down globalization can be perpetuated through various forms of soft power and what role theology plays in this context.

Continuing the trajectory of chapter 1, globalization can still be defined in terms of the expansion of top-down power at all levels of life, of mounting power differentials, of suppression of alternatives at all levels, and in terms of a concomitant erasure of local difference (both cultural and ecological). Once again, the goal of this sort of globalization is control over as much of the world and as large a part of reality as possible. Even many of the key results of globalization remain the same, as once again the gap between those on top and those on the bottom is growing— this time perhaps more rapidly than ever before. Top-down globalization, whatever its particular creeds and mission statements, continues to create concentrations of power and wealth in the hands of a few, to the detriment of the majority of people.

Whereas the examples for globalization in terms of soft power are drawn more from modern times, there are ancient examples as well. In Christian theology, for instance, it has become commonplace for several generations of theologians to talk about "Hellenization," understood as a purely cultural matter. In this account, power does not appear to play much of a role as early Christian thought is transposed from Palestine into the Hellenistic world, and as its major ideas are reshaped by Hellenistic categories. According to the standard account, it all seems to be a matter of translation aimed at making the Jewish world of the earliest Christian beginnings understood in another cultural context, where people not only speak the Greek language but also think in terms of Greek philosophical categories.

What is overlooked by those who talk about the process of the Hellenization of Christianity in this way, however, is that the Hellenistic traditions were not universal but were the traditions of the upper classes of the Roman Empire. At stake were not merely philosophical debates, or the transposition of ideas between different cultures, but the question of power: who would hold the power to assimilate the budding Christianity to their worldview, and who would be able to use it to further their models of globalization? The divide here is not so much between "Jews" and "Greeks" in general; the divide is between lower and upper classes. "Hellenization" in this context meant to suppress the ways of thinking characteristic of the lower classes in favor of the worldview of the upper classes.[2]

Able to rely on a clear differential of power that was backed up by the Roman Empire, Hellenization did not need to make use of hard power. Hellenization, proceeding via soft power rather than hard power, could act as if its presuppositions were universal. The definitions of humanity and divinity presupposed by the Council of Chalcedon in 451, for instance, reflect this context: Christ is confessed as fully "human" and fully "divine" in seemingly generic fashion, without the need to explain what it means to be human or divine. There is, of course, no generic humanity and divinity, and so it is not surprising that these categories were ultimately shaped according to the ideals of those in charge. Consequently, the images of classical theism as fostered by empire prevailed once again, with all their top-down imagery. As a result, a more appropriate alternative definition of humanity and divinity in terms of the life and ministry of Jesus, with all its support for bottom-up models, was suppressed. Top-down globalization won this war without shedding a single drop of blood.

Our next example for a link between theology and globalization that proceeds via soft power is Bartolomé de Las Casas. His work demonstrates the sort of ambivalence highlighted by postcolonial theorists. Although he rejected the harsh methods of the Spanish conquest, Las Casas continued to support the interests of the Spanish crown in the New World. As a result, Las Casas never fully deconstructed the power differentials on which Spanish top-down globalization rested—in fact, he continued to presuppose these power differentials in his own alternative approach to globalization. Although Las Casas did a lot of good—he was, after all, able to challenge and reverse some of the worst consequences of the conquest—his approach nevertheless

35

spearheaded the softer forms of colonialism embodied in later European colonial history. And although he paved the way for the recognition of the basic humanity of the Indians and their sacred worth, he never gave up the assumption that Christian Spanish culture was superior and more advanced.

Whereas Las Casas challenged the use of hard power against the Indians (though not against other nations), he did not challenge the Spanish Empire when it proceeded via soft power. His notion of the "way of Christ" modeled such soft power, guiding Spanish efforts to shape and reshape the lives and traditions of the Indians. As a result, the Indians were made more pliable to Spanish interests by the missionaries' demonstration of love, care, and support. While Christ does not work through violence—forgetting this was the mistake of the conquistadors, Las Casas believed—Las Casas assumed that Christ works through a sort of persuasion that is irresistible and that guarantees that the Spanish Empire will succeed. Las Casas did not harbor the slightest doubt that, if given free choice, the Indians would come to support Spain and its purposes: the reason for his confidence was the deep-seated assumption of the inherent superiority of the Spanish Christians over all others, especially when they embody the "way of Christ," which is gentle and caring.

In this context, the radical erasure of the local proves to be harmful. Local differences are welcome, as long as they help keep the people happy and productive. Las Casas envisioned that certain cultural differences should be allowed to flourish, and that the Indians, though working for the Spaniards, should be allowed to remain in their communities where they could maintain some of their traditional ways of life. What needed to be erased were only those differences that stood in contradiction to the goals and the values of the Spanish, which, in Las Casas's estimate were few. He assumed that the Indians were simply less developed, but on the right track. Nevertheless, while Las Casas acknowledged the differences of the Indians and studied them—including their languages—he was quite clear that whenever there was a clash between Christian Spanish and Indian culture, the former must prevail.

Las Casas's approach is located at the threshold of modernity. The Spanish conquest and its consequences are closely related to the onset of modernity in Europe, as Enrique Dussel and other Latin American thinkers have pointed out. Modern Europe develops in relation to its colonial others, rather than on the basis of its own grandeur, as has commonly been assumed. Going beyond this basic observation, this interpretation is also supported by the little-known fact that Las Casas became one of the heroes of modern northern European colonialism—a colonialism that was quite proud of its more enlightened ways and which rejected what now seemed to be the barbaric and unnecessarily violent methods of the Spanish conquest.

Friedrich Schleiermacher, the nineteenth-century father of modern theology writing in Prussia, also promoted a form of soft power, which he felt was superior to hard power. Christ is modeling this sort of power, Schleiermacher observed, since he works not through coercion but through attraction. This theological interpretation set the stage for an even more refined model of globalization via soft power. Schleiermacher firmly believed that these forces of attraction would produce results in all areas—religious, cultural, political, and economic—because he took for granted that superior cultures (like the Christian ones) were irresistible to what he considered to be lower cultures. The world would have been Christianized already in his time, Schleiermacher argued, were it not for the fact that the missionaries worked through force and coercion, and thus turned people against them.

Schleiermacher's work needs to be seen in the context of European colonialism. Although Prussia did not have colonies at the time when Schleiermacher wrote in the early decades of the nineteenth century, the German-speaking countries were consumed by what has been called a "colonial fantasy." Rejecting not only the violence and force of the Spanish conquest, the Germans also rejected Dutch and British models of colonialism—the former because they saw it as cold and the latter because they saw it as driven by greed. The German colonial fantasy was linked to the idea of education: Germans would share their knowledge and insight with others, raising them closer to their level of education and civilization. The power of education that is promoted here might be seen as the ultimate example of soft power—gentle, yet firmly rooted in notions of cultural supe- riority. To be sure, those who promoted this process did not see it in terms of power, but a differential of power between Germans and others was presupposed nevertheless. This differential of power provided the dynamic that would have made the relation- ship work.

According to Schleiermacher, the success of Christianity, like the success of future German colonialism, rests in its attractive power. Presupposing an inbuilt superiority, this power does not need to be defended anxiously. Schleiermacher's take on miracles expresses the overall spirit that drives his work: "Even if it can- not be strictly proved that the Church's power of working mira- cles has died out . . . yet in general it is undeniable that, in view of the great advantage in power and civilization which the Christian peoples possess over the non-Christian . . . the preach- ers of to-day do not need such signs."[3] Christianity and German civilization did not need to rely on divine miracles anymore because they were the embodiment of the divine miracle: their power and civilization embodied the divine power on earth.

Schleiermacher exemplifies what Edward Said has called "Orientalism" and what Walter Mignolo has called "Occidentalism": Europe develops its own self-understanding and a sense of its own value by distinguishing itself from others.[4] The Middle Eastern (oriental) or Latin American (occidental) others become the foils on which the European self understands itself. In the process, images of, and ideas about, others help shore up the European self, as the others are being stereotyped and roman- ticized. These processes often take place without direct violence or the use of hard power, as the European self is convinced that it has the best interests of others in mind. Nevertheless, the flow of power is clear: Orientalism and Occidentalism function on the basis of a significant differential of power.

The postcolonial empire, a contradiction in terms at first sight, is based on these more enlightened forms of colonialism and on persistent Orientalisms and Occidentalisms. As the colonial world, with its established structures of top-down power embodied by colonial governments and standing armies, comes to an end, power differentials are maintained in different ways. Postcolonial models of globalization seem to have taken to heart an insight by Adam Smith that colonialism was too cumbersome, that its heavy-handed superstructure was too expensive, and that it was therefore not very profitable for the colonizers. Globalization in postcolonial times seems to have learned some of the lessons of Las Casas and Schleiermacher, in particular that—especially in a situation of pronounced power differentials—global domination and control can be achieved more effectively through soft power than through hard.

In the context of clear global power differentials, theology tends to affiliate itself with dominant processes of globalization and the mostly economic and cultural processes that undergird them. The so-called gospel of prosperity, for instance, proclaims that anyone who seeks to follow Jesus and who commits to the discipline of the churches that promote prosperity will be rewarded with great wealth. The roots of this approach run deep, so the gospel of prosperity cannot be dismissed as a mere fad. Identifying God with positions at the top of the spectrum of wealth and power is common also in the mainline churches. Because of the dominance of this top-down model in religion— paralleling what is happening in economics and politics—this is the default position of any theology that does not explicitly link its images of God to the "least of these" (Matt. 25:40).

This principle of God at the top is at work even in many of those theologies that argue for the support of others in need. Models of charity promoted by local churches, for instance, often assume that others are being helped when they are "lifted up" to become more like the members of the church—economically and culturally. Even advocacy and community-organizing projects often function in this mode, especially when they seek to make sure that others will get their own slice of the "American pie" and thus will endorse the methods by which this pie is baked. On a global level, it is the notion of development that often gives

39

leverage to the idea that God is at the top—with those who are more developed. As my research assistant Kevin Minister pointed out when reading this passage, this can be seen not only economically but also ecclesially in the assumption that missionary movements ought to flow from the United States to the third world—a flow that tends to be the same in both liberal and conservative missions. The task that is commonly agreed on by all these models, therefore, is to raise others up to higher levels defined by those who consider themselves to be at the top. The models of globalization related to these ideas continue to promote the erasure of local differences and the suppression of real alternatives.

The economic confidence that a rising tide will lift all boats might be considered a slightly less church-centered version of the gospel of prosperity. It is this confidence that helps people live through economic recessions and depressions, even though there is less and less evidence that the majority of boats are lifted by the rising tide of the capitalist free-market economy as it has evolved in our times. The soft power embodied by the market demands a strong sort of faith that at times is reminiscent of the pie-in-the-sky faith some forms of religion promote. Yet economic globalization proceeds to demand political deregulation on the basis of this faith, as the free market is supposed to be the ultimate regulator through its "invisible hand" (Adam Smith).[5]

Theological positions supporting such faith span the spectrum: both liberals and conservatives embrace it, manifest in a fundamental optimism about the power of the market. Opus Dei, a conservative Roman Catholic organization, combines an extremely conservative theology and morality with an attitude that welcomes capitalism—they run two of the most prestigious business schools in Spain.[6] At the same time, there is also a growing resistance that can be found in many areas of this spectrum, as we shall see in the next chapter. The culture wars of the United States, between liberals and conservatives, are not as important in this context as has often been assumed: those who have emphasized the conservative nature of Christianity in the Global South tend to overlook that while many Christians in the

South may have strong interests in the Bible, they read differently and the topics tend to be different.[7]

Backed by a religious faith that endorses globalizing capital, economics takes on a special role in driving top-down globalization without being noticed. A particular sort of top-down power is lodged here, because although the postcolonial empire tends to support notions of political democracy, democracy is not a virtue that is promoted at the economic level.[8] The importance of economics, supported by religion, is crucial for understanding the nature of the postcolonial empire. The economic realm is now more global than the realm of the political—demonstrated best by the most recent economic depression, which has reached new global dimensions. The sort of soft power that is a mark of this situation, often at work beneath the surface, is supported by vast differentials in economic standing. That the world is flat (Thomas Friedman) can only be assumed from a position of economic power at the top of the economic world, which lacks full awareness of its own power. Likewise, the question *Why do they hate us so?* raised for instance after the terrorist attacks on September 11, 2001, usually comes from those at the top who are unaware of their location at the top. However, those who look at the United States from behind the fences that are going up on its southern borders have a much different perspective. And even if they manage to cross these fences, thereby risking their lives, the world will not become much flatter for them.

That the world is flat is not only the basic principle of a form of top-down globalization that proceeds via soft power; it is also supported by much of theology.[9] Those who talk about "missionaries in reverse," for instance, assume that this is a fairly straightforward matter. Christians from Africa tend to inspire us and invigorate us with their spirited music and colorful clothes; Christians from Asia impress us by their deep spirituality, and so on. People in the United States and in Europe often talk about how "enriching" these encounters are to them—thus expressing the underlying flow of power: *they* provide a service to *us*. In this climate, local differences are now more accepted than in the past, but only insofar as they do not challenge the powers that be.

Globalization and Theology

Adding color and enrichment is one thing, providing a challenge is another that does not fit with the idea that the world is flat. In this context, awareness and appreciation of local differences is helpful to the dominant interests, for instance, if it facilitates the expansion of the market economy into uncharted territory and inspires the advertising industry.

In the process, local differences are often reduced to matters of folklore and style that do not challenge the system. Talk about "inculturation," for example, including the inculturation of the gospel in faraway places on the mission field, usually does not imply a challenge to the already established versions of the gospel back home. As a result, top-down power is not affected by this process. Viewed from this angle, nevertheless, globalization appears to be evolving: while it continues to be about global expansion, it is no longer about the erasure of difference—as long as difference remains trivial. Here is a parallel to certain post-modern forms of appreciation for otherness and difference, which often exhaust themselves in differences of taste without posing a challenge to anyone. Consequently, top-down power is not only left without a challenge, but is empowered and authorized to extend its control to ever-farther regions of the globe.

GLOBALIZATION AND THEOLOGIES PROVIDING ALTERNATIVES TO SOFT POWER

The British Empire considered itself to be a civilized affair, promoting not untempered force and violence but trade relations and political treatises. For the longest time, the British were present in places like India through trading posts, which eventually grew into the British East India Company. Only in the middle of the nineteenth century did the British take political control of India, after a nationwide insurrection, which became known as India's First War of Independence. Apart from a few blemishes, like the British participation in the transatlantic slave trade, the British would have considered themselves to be in the business of the improvement of humanity.

Nevertheless, there were clear power differentials at work here, with established top-down relationships at all levels. Those who wanted to make it up the ladder in England but were of less prominent descent often tried to make it in the colonies first.

This included not only businesspeople but also academics. Religion was part of this top-down flow of power as well. In this context, an alternative approach promoted by John Wesley, an eighteenth-century theologian and the founder of Methodism, was quite unexpected. According to Wesley, "Religion must not go from the greatest to the least, or the power would appear to be of men."[1] The first thing to be noted here is that Wesley perceives a flow of power in religion, an issue that would hardly occur to many theologians and church people even today. This flow of power in religion parallels the flow of power in top-down processes of globalization, even if they proceed via soft power rather than hard.

What set Wesley apart from the theology of his time was that he came to realize that religion could indeed go the other way around—starting not from the top down but from the bottom up. This was not just a radical idea of a great mind; this idea was closely connected to the emergence of an alternative religious movement with globalizing promise—early Methodism—whose dynamic depended on its relation to common people and members of the working class, who would become leaders of their own movement and who began to shape their own destiny. That is the deeper meaning of the otherwise worn-out notion of Wesley as "folk theologian." That Wesley could translate complex theological concepts for common people certainly contributed to the movement; but the much more interesting question is how this connection with common people shaped Wesley's own theology and how the particular forms of Methodism that flow from this— an alternative form of globalization—are tied to this emerging bottom-up dynamic.

In the midst of the dominant forms of globalization of Wesley's day, moving "from the greatest to the least," from the British Empire's trade relations with the colonies and from the emerging captains of industry to the factory floors (where workers were no longer indentured servants but wage-earning employees), Wesley identified a different process. If the divine were found primarily not at the top but at the bottom of the world, theology might indeed move "from the least to the greatest," from the bottom up.

This bottom-up movement can be seen in Wesley's work, when he appointed preachers who were uneducated working people and when he included women, but it can also be seen in his theology. Picking up a common strand that was present under the surface of his life's work, the later Wesley incorporated what he called "works of mercy" into the classical Anglican list of the means of grace (prayer, Bible study, Holy Communion). Engaging those on the bottom of society, therefore, becomes a "channel" of God's grace, a way in which God engages the church and transforms it.[2] Meeting the divine at the bottom, with those in need, rebuilds the life of faith from the bottom up. This movement that is characteristic of God's grace in many of the Judeo-Christian traditions—from the bottom up instead of from the top down—translates into an alternative process of globalization, which might be described as "globalization from below."

The various theologies of liberation, which have emerged over the past forty years, can also be seen as providing alternatives to soft forms of top-down globalization. Black theology and feminist theology in the United States, for instance, emerged at a time when the hardest forms of oppression had already been overcome: slavery had been abolished a century earlier in Europe and the United States, and African Americans in the United States had gained some independence and the right to vote. Yet the pressure on African Americans and women was still very real and systemic. The struggle against Jim Crow laws and for increasing the equality of women had to deal with softer forms of power than the struggle against slavery, and this struggle continues today against even softer forms of power. Such softer forms of power now often find expressions in ways that are harder to see, for instance through lower paychecks, hidden prejudices that make it more difficult to get jobs or fair treatment before the law, and even the sort of romanticization that seeks to shape other people according to our fantasies. Men, for example, tend to romanticize women in these ways when they try to make them conform to male images of beauty and womanhood. These problems are exacerbated because of the underlying differentials of power at work, which often take economic form.

The history of Latin American liberation theology provides another example for theological resistance to the soft power of globalization. Many of the misunderstandings of Latin American liberation theology have to do with a failure to understand that this theology emerged in a self-conscious process of resistance to soft power. The dominant model in the Americas and other "third-world countries" in the 1950s and 1960s was the model of development. This was a time of soft power, when the "first-world countries" declared their intentions to help the "third world" through development projects. In this context, the difference between the two settings was understood in terms of development. The more developed countries, the reasoning went, should seek to support the less developed countries so that they, too, could enter into a process of development. This basic approach was backed up, furthermore, by the "theologies of development."

Although the development approach was well intentioned, it contained all the elements of top-down globalization via soft power. The language of development lent itself to the idea that the underdeveloped countries just needed to catch up with the developed ones. The causes of what was seen as underdevelopment were not deemed important to these development projects, although a certain understanding of inferiority was always part of this terminology; either people were underdeveloped because of a lack of intelligence, industry, or character, or they were underdeveloped because of a certain backwardness and lack of education. The transfer of knowledge, technology, industry, capital, and all the other virtues that appeared to make the developed countries superior was supposed to fix these problems. God's favor, which had blessed the developed countries, could now be transferred through development projects, or so it seemed.

Liberation theology made a crucial contribution in this situation as it began to challenge this point of view. The problem, as theologians like Gustavo Gutiérrez, Hugo Assmann, and others pointed out, was not development and underdevelopment as such. The problem had to do with a relationship that permitted some countries to pursue their development on the backs of others who in turn were not only left behind but who were also actively underdeveloped. The differential between the "first world" and the "third world," these theologians came to realize, had to do with a differential of power, which allowed one world to exploit the others for its own purposes. History backs up this interpretation: for centuries, resources extracted from Latin America and other parts of the world funded European development. Furthermore, millions of people who would have been in a position to contribute to their own countries and make history were prevented from doing so by subjugation and slavery, which forced them to work for the benefit of the dominant groups in the dominant countries. Many advanced cultures and their knowledge bases were simply destroyed in the process.

While the so-called dependency theories, which informed some of the early theologies of liberation, were often too broad and somewhat simplistic, they nevertheless provided important insights at various levels: political, economic, cultural, and theological. The images of God that had endorsed the top-down globalization processes of Europe and the United States were called into question in this context. How could the common people in Latin America trust a God who worked for the advantage of others, and in doing so contributed to their own disadvantage? The God of the masters and the God of the people could no longer be considered to be one and the same. Such insights eventually led to a deeper understanding of some matters that were not seen clearly enough by the dependency theorists.

The problem with the dependency theories was that they failed to understand the deeper implications of the soft power of globalization, like the fact that some of the divisions between north and south ran through the North and the South themselves. Not all Europeans and North Americans benefited from an economic arrangement that maintained the dependency of the poor on the wealthy, just as some powerful South Americans and Africans benefited greatly. In this context, liberation theology needed to pay closer attention to the economics and the divisions of class structures within the various contexts—an ongoing challenge that is only now being addressed more fully.[3]

The alternatives that emerge here are real and go deep, which is why liberation theologies have been subject to rabid critiques that border on persecution, which few other theologies have had to endure in modern times. In the 1980s, the Reagan administration declared Latin American liberation theology as a major threat to U.S. interests in the hemisphere, opening the floodgates to a witch-hunt.[4] In the mid 1980s various Latin American liberation theologians were summoned to appear at heresy trials, which began with the Vatican's silencing of Leonardo Boff; as recently as 2007 the Vatican censured several of Jon Sobrino's writings. What distinguishes liberation theologies—whether Latin American or others—from much of mainline theology is that they are tied to liberation movements and thus to masses of people struggling for a better life. Nevertheless, theological reflections are tied to these struggles in a self-critical fashion. The point is not to jump on any bandwagon but to investigate alternative visions of God and the world that are emerging here. In a situation where real alternatives are scarce and repressed both intentionally and unintentionally, this is the only way to develop a different approach.

Liberation theologies, in sync with many of the core Judeo-Christian traditions, find God on the margins, where Godself is struggling with the people for their liberation and a better life. The globalizing thrust that emerges from this observation moves from the bottom up, rather than from the top down. This is one of the most fundamental differences compared to the theology of development, the contemporary gospel of prosperity, and much of current mainline theology, where the globalizing thrust moves from the top down in various ways. Although all these approaches include the hope for material well-being, this difference is absolutely crucial. Philip Jenkins is right that separating spiritual and material well-being is a luxury for those in the North who are wealthy. He is nevertheless wrong when he claims that "the Prosperity Gospel is an inevitable by-product of a church containing so many of the very poorest."[5] Liberation theologies keep providing real alternatives from below.

Two questions emerge here: which of these movements are really contributing to people's well-being, and which of these movements are closer to the heart of the Judeo-Christian traditions? If top-down globalization continues to increase the gap between the rich and the poor, and if even development politics turns out to be good business for the developers to the detriment of those who are supposed to be "developing," it is hard to see how the theology of development or the gospel of prosperity, which celebrates the wealthy and the powerful, can make a real difference in the lives of the multitude.[6] Globalizing moves from the bottom up, however, appear to have a better track record. When workers join trade unions, for instance, it is not only the case that their wages and benefits increase; in areas where unions are strong, even nonunionized workers benefit. When Latin American peasants organize themselves, they often stand a better chance to prevail on their ancestral lands; sometimes they are even able to establish themselves again on unused lands, as the landless movements in Brazil have shown. In this context, emerging coalitions of labor and religion are making a difference that is not yet fully recognized: as Christians begin to side with their downtrodden neighbors, as did Jesus, progress is made on all sides. Pressures of top-down globalization are relieved, new excitement for core traditions of the Christian faith grows, and it is not unheard of that conversions happen in this context.

These reflections bring us to contemporary theological developments. As top-down globalization processes continue, mostly via soft power, alternative processes of globalization from below gather steam. Some of their experiences and insights are paralleled by theological developments. It has been estimated that the number of alternative movements of globalization, working against top-down globalization, is in the millions.[7] When put together, this is the largest movement in history. Unfortunately, much of what is going on goes virtually unreported in the mass media, where most reports about alternative movements focus on a tiny minority that is intent on committing violent acts. What is really under way here, however, is an alternative movement that is constructive and that has developed constructive ways of using some of the tools of dominant globalization in different ways: the internet, for instance, has become a useful tool of organizing from below, as has cell-phone technology through texting and other instant forms of communication.

These movements include a broad range of groups, from the aforementioned landless movements in Brazil, where displaced people settle on uncultivated land and cultivate it for subsistence farming, to more exotic groups like the Guerilla Gardeners in Europe and the United States, where people grow gardens in unusual places like parking lots, golf courses, or neglected land. In both cases, attention is drawn to the fact that capital-driven globalization is closely connected to corporate takeovers of communal lands.[8] Another example of an emerging movement is the current growth of religion and labor coalitions in the United States, which link back to a centuries-old history that has often been forgotten.[9] These groups are addressing the problems created by top-down globalization, like economic injustices and disparities, but many are also mindful of related problems like global warming. In the United States, for example, many evangelical Christians have lately become aware of environmental problems, and because their communities are directly affected, many more around the globe have a sense of the deep problems economic injustices create. Phenomena like environmental racism and other environmental injustices have put the burden disproportionately on those communities that benefit the least from top-down globalization.

Even the churches are not completely disconnected from these developments. This shows that religion can never be limited to the status quo, and Christians and non-Christians are frequently seen working hand in hand in alternative movements. Nevertheless, even those church communities that are open to globalization from the bottom up often display a tendency to neglect some of the more challenging elements of the movement. Seeking to serve suffering people and the damaged natural world is one thing, struggling together with people and nature to overcome the roots of suffering and damage is another. Many churches are happy to denounce issues like greed and consumerism, but the number of churches that dare to point out that the deeper problem has to do with the structure of free-market capitalism, which fosters the accumulation of wealth in the hands of a few and encourages consumerism in order to be able to keep the lines of production going, is much smaller.

There are developments in the field of theology that correspond to the spirit of bottom-up globalization. The first step, in this context, is when theology pays sustained attention to what is going on in the places of tension in the world. To be sure, this is a move that cannot be taken for granted even in the so-called contextual approaches to theology, which often tend to overlook the dangers of soft power. Even the tools of postcolonial theory and subaltern studies that are used in contemporary theology do not guarantee automatic success in this regard; they only become fruitful if they address the deeper tensions of a globalizing world.

In a recent project that is indebted to the spirit of liberation theology but seeks to develop it further, three theological issues are discussed that deserve special attention in the tension between globalization from above and from below: democracy, subjectivity, and transcendence. Even the history of democracy, going back to ancient Greece, resembles soft-power top-down globalization. Those who tended to rule in many democracies were elite groups of citizens (Greek: *demos*); all others were not part of this democracy. This history is reflected in the early history of democracy in the United States, when only white males who held property were entitled to vote. The alternative to such democracies, inspired by Judeo-Christian traditions, would be to advocate for a rule via "laocracy." In the Judeo-Christian traditions the common people (Greek: *laos*) often play a special role. Jesus focused these traditions thus: "Many who are first will be last, and the last will be first" (Mark 10:31). In this context a new subjectivity emerges, which differs from the top-down subjectivity of modern capitalism: subjects are no longer the self-made businesspeople, but rather the ones who share in Christ's struggles, moving from the bottom up through cross and resurrection.

The notion of transcendence takes on new meaning in this context when it encourages transcending a situation that is supposed to be absolute and closed; the alternatives for everyday life that grow out of this give new meaning to transcendence.[10]

For good reason, alternative globalization movements have been called "the world's other superpower" (UN Secretary-General Kofi Annan). Since they are diverse, decentralized, and highly creative, they are not easily suppressed. Neither are they easily fooled by the flow of soft power from the top down, because they represent a truly alternative power. They have an edge that allows them to pose challenges and to "speak truth to power" because they have access to a truth that can only be identified from the perspective of the underside, much like the truth of Christ that is accessible to infants (Matt. 11:25), another marginalized group in the ancient world.[11]

CHAPTER SIX

THEOLOGY AND POWER IN A GLOBALIZING WORLD: THE LESSONS OF GLOBALIZATION AND EMPIRE

A key problem with top-down globalization in terms of the expansion of power, the erasure (or trivialization) of local differences, and the active elimination of alternatives is that it knows no limits. It cannot be restricted to the realm of politics or economics. Instead, this sort of globalization seeks to extend its rule by any means, including cultural and religious, and it does not stop until it has reached the innermost parts of people's personality and the deepest recesses of the natural world. Theology is therefore part and parcel of globalization, whether this is acknowledged or not. Even the most academic efforts of theology are located in the context of the global expansion of power.

As we have seen, throughout its two-thousand-year history Christian theology has never existed in isolation. The history of Christian theology begins with the globalizing efforts of the Roman Empire, using both hard power and soft power, and has been linked to the globalizing efforts of empires ever since. Globalization as expansion of top-down power, erasure of difference, and the elimination of alternatives is ultimately about empire—that is, about the ever-greater control of the world and of our lives. For this reason, we can no longer afford to limit the study of theology to the study of "theology and culture," or "Christ and culture," as H. Richard Niebuhr did in a book by that title, which is still widely in use. Today we need to talk about "theology plus culture plus power," or "Christ plus culture plus power."[1] Theology never exists in a vacuum of power. Not addressing the question of power—like not addressing the question of politics—amounts to endorsing by default the powers that be. As a result, talk about globalization or empire must become part of the standard vocabulary of all theology.

Addressing the question of power, however, does not mean looking at power merely in a negative light. Dealing with the question of power aims at developing the capacity to conceive of alternatives. If theology in a globalizing world does not want to become simply an appendage of powerful top-down processes of globalization, we need to make use of our resources as fully as possible. In Christian theology, a new level of engagement with the biblical sources and the resources of the Christian tradition might have the potential to point us in the right direction. Although the historical-critical study of the Bible has provided many helpful insights, the question is now what it might mean to study the Bible in what I have called a "historical *self*-critical" mode.[2]

The same is true for the way we study the abundance of resources of the Christian tradition. The work of interpretation and hermeneutics can no longer be approached in the illusionary isolation of academic ivory towers. Interpreting ancient and contemporary elements of the Christian tradition in light of the pressures of the globalization at work in their times will expose many parallels. Neither Jesus, Paul, nor Bartolomé de Las Casas can be understood if it is overlooked that they were wrestling with the top-down powers of globalization in their own time, and that they managed to connect with alternative forms of globalization and power and to propose real alternatives. Without this awareness we will not be able to identify their contribution in the midst of contemporary struggles in a globalizing world.

How might current practices of globalization be challenged in a historical self-critical fashion, for instance, by a fresh understanding of Jesus? The question is not merely what Jesus would do, but what Jesus would *not* do. What sorts of things would Jesus reject? This is the form that the Beatitudes take in Luke's Gospel: "Blessed are you . . ."; "But woe to you . . ." (Luke 6:20-26). This is also the form of confession used in the Barmen Declaration of the German Confessing Church in 1934, in resisting Hitler and the political and religious leaders of Nazi Germany. When Christians confess Jesus as "the one Word of God," as Barmen did, what do they reject? Barmen's rejection was directed at those who claimed to represent the Word of God at the time—a clear critique of Hitler and his endorsement by the so-called "German Christians."

This form of assertion and rejection can also be found in ancient Christian confessions, but is frequently neglected by present-day confessing movements. The question today is not merely whether Christians confess the Trinity or the divinity of Christ. The question is what these confessions mean in their respective contexts of globalization in terms of top-down power. For example, what would it mean to reject the idea that there is a hierarchy in the relations of the three divine persons, which is one of the implications of trinitarian doctrine as formulated in the Nicene Creed? Would this not imply a rejection of hierarchical models of globalization, whether through hard power or through soft power, as they are embodied in religious communities and in the world at large?

This sort of self-critical theological reflection has the potential to turn the processes of top-down globalization upside down. One example is the theological problem of the relation between different religions, a challenge that cannot be avoided in a globalizing world. In our time, the hard-power approach of complete rejection or subjection of other religions makes less and less sense as people of different faiths live in ever greater proximity; but neither does the sort of interreligious dialogue make sense where religious people and theologians sit around a table and talk about religious ideas without considering the differentials of power that continue to shape the interrelations of religions in a globalizing world. Keep in mind that if religions emerged in the force fields of globalization and empire, so did interreligious encounters. History is full of examples—whether we think of Christian-Muslim relations during the Crusades in the Middle Ages, Christian-Muslim relations at the beginning of modernity in Spain, the many centuries of Christian-Jewish relations in Europe, or the constructions of Hinduism developed by Christian European scholars in the nineteenth century.

In this context, well-meaning approaches to interreligious dialogue that seek to identify some underlying values that all religions share must now be understood as part of the problem—they function too much in terms of soft-power globalization from above and the related erasure of local differences. Interreligious dialogue in the force field of globalization will be more fruitful for all involved if we begin to deal with it in light of the real-life tensions introduced by the dominant forms of top-down globalization. Genuine interreligious exchanges require a self-critical understanding of one's own heritage as it is linked with the power dynamics of globalization. To be sure, the goal of it all is not negative but positive: this approach will help us identify alternative forms of globalization from the bottom up that already exist beneath the surface in many religious traditions, and it will help us establish interreligious relationships on this basis in new ways.

In doing this sort of self-critical work, theology is not without support. The newly emerging field of cultural studies is of interest, for instance, because it allows us to study not only culture in all its complexity but also how power flows through culture and how it is perpetuated by it. Furthermore, the emerging field of subaltern studies, an approach developed initially in India and

Latin America, has developed new ways of studying what is going on in the lives of people who are pushed to the underside of society—to the "subaltern," which is the location of the dangerous sort of local differences that are facing erasure by top-down globalization. The important question, in this context, is not simply how these local differences could be preserved, but how they could become sources for real alternatives by which different processes of globalization from below are initiated. Subaltern studies are linked to liberation theologies, which have called our attention to these matters for several decades now.[3]

The welcome news is that these approaches are not just dreams for the future but are embodied in actual movements on the ground, from which they draw energy and epistemological support. New sorts of interfaith dialogues, for instance, have manifested new dynamics in religious communities. The interfaith dialogues that are most exciting today take place where religious communities work together on specific projects that resist globalization from the top down and promote real alternatives like the Chicago-based Interfaith Worker Justice (IWF) and the religion and labor groups that work under the umbrella of Jobs with Justice (JWJ). Here local differences of faith are not dissolved but employed, as various resources are brought together in a common struggle that engages the divine in our time. In these settings, matters of theology are not bracketed but are being discussed with new energy in a new context where religious communities contribute to a different sort of globalization from below.

Theology in a globalizing world is confronted with a choice. Does it continue with business as usual in its various forms—pursuing the default mode of globalization, which moves from the top down? Or does it pursue a different dynamic, which in the Christian traditions is modeled by Jesus' birth, life, ministry, death, and resurrection? Unfortunately, many Christians assume that Jesus' life and ministry was only a temporary fix and that the resurrected Christ who "sits at the right hand of God" has joined forces with a different sort of power than that which was manifest in his life. In this way, the subversive parts of the Judeo-Christian traditions are domesticated, including the Jesus traditions. This approach also betrays Paul's notion of the scandal of the cross and the paradoxical power that is made perfect in weakness, of which he testified (1 Cor. 1:23-25; 2 Cor. 12:8-9). It further betrays one of the basic themes of the Judeo-Christian traditions, namely, that God takes a stand against the powerful and with the humble and the meek—a position best summarized by Hannah and Mary (1 Sam. 2:1-10; Luke 1:46-56).

In theological circles, the spirit of globalization from above is sometimes justified because it appears to combat relativism, a situation where "anything goes" and truth no longer exists. If an elite group at the top gets to determine what is true for everyone, then the danger of relativism appears to be held in check. What is overlooked here, however, is that such arrangements are never able to achieve true universality. The only thing that is achieved here is the universalization of a particular relativity, namely the relativity of the elite. Relativism cannot now, nor could it ever be, overcome from the top down. That is one of the fundamental theological problems with which Christianity has to wrestle in a world under the pressures of top-down globalization.

A better response to the problem of relativism can be developed when starting the other way around. When globalization is pursued from below, it is possible to own up to one's relativity without having to remain stuck there. As differences are openly negotiated with others in a situation where no one is in a position of overarching power, a new form of community emerges— a sort of unity in difference—that leads us beyond the traps of relativism. This is the way many of the biblical and traditional texts of Christianity tend to deal with relativity. The plurality of voices in the Bible and the Christian traditions reminds us that a truly global vision does not mean the kind of unity where everyone says exactly the same thing. Nevertheless, this plurality does not mean that all things are relative and that anything goes. Broader perspectives and truly global visions emerge when all these different voices—the many different books of the Bible written by different communities and authors over long periods of time, and the many voices of the Christian tradition, especially the ones that are easily forgotten today—come together and inform one another in light of the common pain and the struggles of life. In this sense, the cross of Jesus Christ—put on his shoulders by the top-down globalizers of his own day—and the many crosses that humans have been forced to bear ever since, point to a new reality and to a new community that emerges from the bottom up. In the words of the apostle Paul: "If one member suffers, all suffer together with it" (1 Cor. 12:26).

IN A GLOBALIZING WORLD, THE MIDDLE ROAD LEADS TO DEATH

Ulrich Beck is right when he points out that "globality means that from now on nothing which happens on our planet is only a limited local event."[1] This can be good news or bad news, depending on what is about to be globalized, and by which methods something is globalized. In order to come to understand the good news of globalization we need to confront the bad news. We need to face the current darkness in order to understand where the light is shining brightly. The good news is that there are alternative models to globalization from above, that these models cannot easily be suppressed, and that these alternatives are deeply linked to some of our religious traditions, past and present.

But is this really a question of either-or? Is there no middle road between the extremes of a dominant globalization from above and alternatives from below? What if it was the role of theology to find a neutral middle ground, instead of taking sides and getting involved? After all, is Christianity not called to be "in the world, but not of the world" (cf. John 17:6-19)? An old German proverb states that in situations of danger and great need, the middle road leads to death (in Gefahr und grosser Not bringt der Mittelweg den Tod [Friedrich von Logau]). The problem is that in situations of grave power differentials, such as the present one, there is no place of neutrality and no middle road. The German reformer Martin Luther knew in his own way that there is no middle road when he described the human will as a horse or a donkey (Reittier), which is ridden either by the devil or by God.

No place is safe from globalization as the progressive expansion of power and the erasure of differences and alternatives, and no place is safe from the related growth in the gaps in wealth and in power. The dominant form of globalization in our own time, it turns out, does not promote a leveling process, just as it is becoming clearer every day that a rising tide does not lift all boats. This dominant form of globalization affects all aspects of life; no place is safe, neither at the ends of the earth nor at home. We are not even safe in the privacy of our communities, or in our own minds and souls. Consequently, there is no neutral place in the middle, as those who seek to hang out there are quickly pulled, for the most part without even noticing, in the direction of the greater force that does not allow for alternatives. Recall also that those who in past manifestations of globalization had attempted to pursue the middle road often discovered too late that they were drawn into the maelstrom of the dominant status quo. The churches in Nazi Germany that sought to stay out of politics and retreated into their own private spheres are among the sad examples.

What is ultimately at stake for theology is how the divine is envisioned. Core traditions of Judaism, Christianity, and many other religions keep pointing us to the margins and to the bottom. In the Christian traditions this is where God becomes human— at work in Christ, who lives as a construction worker and organizer; and it is from there that the good news of the gospel moves into the world and around the globe, to the ends of the earth—a true process of globalization from below that ends up reaching all the way to the top and transforming things. In this process, local differences are not erased but make much-needed contributions to the whole, informing new kinds of power from below. Likewise, those who are pushed to the margins by the current dynamics of top-down globalization—the majority of humanity—are no longer the passive recipients of the schemes of globalization. They are the ones who set the stage for a new kind of community and new processes of globalization, because they understand the profound meaning of the Apostle Paul's insight that if one member of the community suffers, all suffer together with it.

The problem of theology and globalization is, therefore, neither theology nor globalization as such. It all depends on what kind of theology and what kind of globalization is promoted, how the two feed into each other, and which model corresponds best with the reality of the divine. A choice has to be made and a stand has to be taken.

NOTES

Introduction

1. David Held and Anthony McGrew, eds., *The Global Transformations Reader: An Introduction to the Globalization Debate* (Cambridge: Polity Press, 2000), 6.

1. Globalization, Theology, and Hard Power

1. This is the basic definition of *empire* that is developed in Joerg Rieger, *Christ and Empire: From Paul to Postcolonial Times* (Minneapolis: Fortress Press, 2007), and Joerg Rieger, "Christian Theology and Empires," in *Empire and the Christian Tradition: New Readings of Classical Theologians*, ed. Kwok Pui-lan, Don H. Compier, and Joerg Rieger (Minneapolis: Fortress Press, 2007).

2. See Richard Horsley, *Jesus and Empire: The Kingdom of God and the New World Disorder* (Minneapolis: Fortress Press, 2003), 33–34.

3. James Scott, *Domination and the Arts of Resistance: Hidden Transcripts* (New Haven: Yale University Press, 1992).

4. See the account in Rieger, *Christ and Empire*, chapter 2.

5. See Gustavo Gutiérrez, *Las Casas: In Search of the Poor of Jesus Christ*, trans. Robert Barr (Maryknoll, N.Y.: Orbis Books, 1993), 461–62.

6. Consider, for instance, Article 4 of the Barmen Declaration: " 'You know that the rulers of the Gentiles lord it over them, and their great men exercise authority over them. It shall not be so among you; but whoever would be great among you must be your servant' (Matt. 20:25, 26). The various offices in the Church do not establish a dominion of some over the others; on the contrary, they are for the exercise of the ministry entrusted to and enjoined upon the whole congregation. We reject the false doctrine, as though the Church, apart from this ministry, could and were permitted to give itself, or allow to be given to it, special leaders vested with ruling powers." On the web: www.sacred-texts.com/chr/barmen.htm.

7. Karl Heim, *Jesus der Herr: Die Führervollmacht Jesu und die Gottesoffenbarung in Christus* (Berlin: Furche Verlag, 1935), 77 (my translation).

2. Globalization and Theologies Providing Alternatives to Hard Power

1. The link between social and ecological relations is developed by David Harvey, "What Is Green and Makes the Environment Go Round?" in *The Cultures of Globalization*, ed. Fredric Jameson and Masao Miyoshi (Durham, N.C.: Duke University Press, 1998), 327–55.

2. Richard Horsley, *Jesus and Empire: The Kingdom of God and the New World Disorder* (Minneapolis: Fortress Press, 2003), 54. Note the difference of this approach to other efforts to address the question of the historical Jesus, as Horsley seeks to examine the social nexus in which Jesus works and not only his intellectual legacy.

3. See also the work of Neil Elliott, John Dominic Crossan, and Richard Horsley on Paul.

4. This is no longer the "red pastor of Safenwil" but the "mature" Barth. Karl Barth, *Church Dogmatics* II/1, ed. G. W. Bromiley and T. F. Torrance, trans. T. H. L. Parker et al. (New York: Charles Scribner's Sons, 1957), 386. Compare also Karl Barth, *Church Dogmatics* III/4, ed. G. W. Bromiley and T. F. Torrance, trans. A. T. Mackay et al. (Edinburgh: T & T Clark, 1961), 544, where he states that the "command of God" is "a call for the championing of the weak against every kind of encroachment on the part of the strong." Christianity, therefore, needs to keep itself "to the 'left' in opposition to its champions, i.e., to confess that it is fundamentally on the side of the victims."

5. Dietrich Bonhoeffer, "Der Blick von unten," in *Gesammelte Schriften*, vol. 2 (Munich: Chr. Kaiser, 1959), 441, translation mine.

6. Gustavo Gutiérrez, *The Power of the Poor in History*, trans. Robert R. Barr (Maryknoll, N.Y.: Orbis, 1992), 222–34, refers to Bonhoeffer. See also the work of Ulrich Duchrow in Germany, and the international contributions in Joerg Rieger, ed., *Opting for the Margins: Postmodernity and Liberation in Christian Theology*, American Academy of Religion, Reflection and Theory in the Study of Religion (New York: Oxford University Press, 2003).

7. See Eberhard Bethge, *Dietrich Bonhoeffer: Man of Vision, Man of Courage* (New York: Harper & Row, 1970), 771.

3. Interlude

1. This is the approach taken in *The Postcolonial Studies Reader*, ed. Bill Ashcroft, Gareth Griffiths, and Helen Tiffin (London: Routledge, 1995).

2. See Joerg Rieger, *Christ and Empire: From Paul to Postcolonial Times* (Minneapolis: Fortress Press, 2007), chapter 7.

3. For the terms *hybridity* and *mimicry*, see Homi Bhabha, *The Location of Culture* (London: Routledge, 1994).

4. See, for instance, the account by Naomi Klein, *The Shock Doctrine: The Rise of Disaster Capitalism* (New York: Metropolitan Books, 2007), 325–82.

5. See Kai Nielsen, *Globalization and Justice* (New York: Humanity Books, 2003), 33 and n. 44.

6. For some numbers, see Joerg Rieger, *No Rising Tide: Theology, Economics, and the Future* (Minneapolis: Fortress Press, 2009), chapter 2; see this same chapter for a more succinct definition of class in terms of power. This definition of class in terms of power contradicts an observation by Peter Singer, *One World: The Ethics of Globalization*, 2nd ed. (New Haven: Yale University Press, 2004), 84, who claims that "inequality is not significant in itself. It matters because of the impact it has on welfare."

7. This is an observation by Arif Dirlik, referenced in Rebecca Todd Peters, *In Search of the Good Life: The Ethics of Globalization* (New York: Continuum, 2004), 141.

8. Fredric Jameson, preface to *The Cultures of Globalization*, ed. Fredric Jameson and Masao Miyoshi (Durham, N.C.: Duke University Press, 1998), xii.

4. Globalization, Theology, and Soft Power

1. Bob Roberts Jr., *Glocalization: How Followers of Jesus Engage the New Flat World* (Grand Rapids: Zondervan, 2007), 18. The United States at the time of the Vietnam War, Roberts writes, "failed to understand . . . that wars could be won by free enterprise, thought, and engagement more than expensive bullets and bombardment." Furthermore: "Everyone hates American bullets but loves American dollars!" While Thomas L. Friedman, *The Lexus and the Olive Tree: Understanding Globalization* (New York: Anchor Books, 2000), 46, notes that power is at work in this process—American power rather than British power, which dominated the previous era of globalization—he talks about a process of flattening the world in which the world comes together "as a single, integrated plain." For that reason, talk of first or second or third world gives way to the "Fast World" and the "Slow World."

2. According to Eduardo Hoornaert, *The Memory of the Christian People* (Maryknoll, N.Y.: Orbis Books, 1988), 122–23, as they tried to perfect Christianity through higher cognition, theologians like Clement of Alexandria and Origen did away with an earlier Christian appreciation for the knowledge of lower classes in matters of faith. Irenaeus, Justin, and Tertullian, however, maintained an appreciation for the knowledge of the common people.

3. Friedrich Schleiermacher, *The Christian Faith*, ed. H. R. Mackintosh and J. S. Stewart (Edinburgh: T & T Clark, 1986), 450.

4. Edward Said, *Orientalism* (New York: Pantheon Books, 1978); Walter Mignolo, *Local Histories, Global Design: Coloniality, Subaltern Knowledges, and Border Thinking* (Princeton, N.J.: Princeton University Press, 2000).

5. See the interpretations of Adam Smith, including the reference on his critique of colonialism, in Joerg Rieger, *No Rising Tide: Theology, Economics, and the Future* (Minneapolis: Fortress Press, 2009).

6. Referenced in *Many Globalizations: Cultural Diversity in the Contemporary World*, ed. Peter L. Berger and Samuel P. Huntington (New York: Oxford University Press, 2002), 12.

7. Philip Jenkins, *The New Faces of Christianity: Believing the Bible in the Global South* (New York: Oxford University Press, 2006), appears to be extending the North American culture wars into this situation when he likens southern Christians' strong interest in the Bible to that of conservative Christians in the North, in contrast with more liberal stances. Although he offers a caveat that these terms do not apply directly (p. 12), the discussion of the book as a whole is framed in terms of the culture wars when he notes that southern literal readings would promote "horror" in American and European liberals and "delight" in the conservatives (p. 2). The core problem is that Jenkins is not always very clear that the topics of concern are different: globally southern Christians do not always read like globally northern conservatives, and literal readings in the South include the concerns of liberation theology rather than a narrow concern for the gospel of prosperity.

8. See also the observation of Rebecca Todd Peters, *In Search of the Good Life: The Ethics of Globalization* (New York: Continuum, 2004), 23: "With the rise of corporate power . . . and financial power . . . the democratic gains that accompanied modernity are slipping away." This comment observes the core challenge but may be too optimistic about modern democracy.

9. Friedman's approach is taken as a key insight in the recent book *Globalizing Theology: Belief and Practice in an Era of World Christianity*, ed. Craig Ott and Harold A. Netland (Grand Rapids: Baker Academic, 2006). See especially the introduction by Netland.

5. Globalization and Theologies Providing Alternatives to Soft Power

1. *The Works of the Rev. John Wesley*, 3rd ed., ed. Thomas Jackson (London: Wesleyan Methodist Book Room, 1872; reprint, Peabody, Mass.: Hendrickson, 1986), 3:178.

2. For an interpretation of Wesley's insistence that works of mercy are means of grace, and the extraordinary consequences for Christianity and Methodism, see Joerg Rieger, *Grace Under Pressure: Negotiating the Heart of the Methodist Traditions*, forthcoming from The General Board of Higher Education, The United Methodist Church, 2011.

3. See, for instance, the work of Jung Mo Sung for a Latin American perspective and Joerg Rieger, *No Rising Tide: Theology, Economics, and the Future* (Minneapolis: Fortress Press, 2009) for a perspective from the United States and Europe.

4. The Committee of Santa Fe, *A New Inter-American Policy for the Eighties* (Washington, D.C.: Council for Inter-American Security, 1980).

5. Philip Jenkins, *The New Faces of Christianity: Believing the Bible in the Global South* (New York: Oxford University Press, 2006), 94.

6. The term *multitude* has been developed by Michael Hardt and Antonio Negri, *Multitude: War and Democracy in the Age of Empire* (New York: Penguin Press, 2004).

7. See Paul Hawken, *Blessed Unrest: How the Largest Social Movement in History Is Restoring Grace, Justice, and Beauty to the World* (New York: Penguin Books, 2007), 2; numbers and descriptions can be found in the more-than-one-hundred-page-long appendix to this book.

8. Many of these stories are recorded in the book *We Are Everywhere: The Irresistible Rise of Global Anticapitalism*, ed. Notes from Nowhere (London: Verso, 2003). In the foreword, Naomi Klein writes: "This book is not just about the movements; it is genuinely of these movements in the best possible way."

9. See, for instance, the work of the organizations Interfaith Worker Justice and Jobs with Justice. A good deal of information can be found on their respective websites: www.iwj.org and www.jwj.org.

10. See Néstor Míguez, Joerg Rieger, and Jung Mo Sung, *Beyond the Spirit of Empire: New Reflections in Politics and Theology*, Reclaiming Liberation Theology Series (London: SCM Press, 2009).

11. Sharon Delgado, *Shaking the Gates of Hell: Faith-Led Resistance to Corporate Globalization* (Minneapolis: Fortress Press, 2007), 226, describes the global justice movement as "decentralized, diverse, creative, and engaged in various struggles around the world"; Hawken, *Blessed Unrest*, 25, talks about "infrapower," a "stirring from below" that resembles the immune system of the human body, identifying what is detrimental to human flourishing. This power is decentralized, working in diverse ways, eliminating what does not affirm and contribute to life (although Hawken does not say much about elimination). For a reflection on the truth that emerges from the underside, see Joerg Rieger, *Remember the Poor: The Challenge to Theology in the Twenty-First Century* (Harrisburg, Pa.: Trinity Press International, 1998), 227–29.

6. Theology and Power in a Globalizing World

1. This is my challenge to H. Richard Niebuhr, *Christ and Culture* (New York: Harper & Brothers, 1956), as posed in Joerg Rieger, *Christ and Empire: From Paul to Postcolonial Times* (Minneapolis: Fortress Press, 2007), vii. A

deeper concern for the study of power is missing in much of theology. The standard concern for culture leaves out the analysis of power. For such a standard definition see Peter L. Berger and Samuel P. Huntington, eds., *Many Globalizations: Cultural Diversity in the Contemporary World* (New York: Oxford University Press, 2001), 2, who understand culture "as the beliefs, values, and lifestyles of ordinary people in their everyday existence."

2. See Rieger, *Christ and Empire*, 8–9, 315.

3. See, for example, John Beverley, *Subalternity and Representation: Arguments in Cultural Theory* (Durham, N.C.: Duke University Press, 1999).

Conclusion

1. Ulrich Beck, "What Is Globalization?" in *The Global Transformations Reader: An Introduction to the Globalization Debate*, ed. David Held and Anthony McGrew (Cambridge: Polity Press, 2000), 102. Beck argues that this is irreversible.

59398934R00046

Made in the USA
Lexington, KY
04 January 2017